TIME FOR KIDS®

CONFIDENT 3 READER

Science Scoops

Spiders!

By the Editors of TIME FOR KIDS
WITH NICOLE IORIO

HarperCollins*Publishers*

About the Author: Nicole Iorio has worked as a writer, editor, and teacher. As a teacher, she loves having kids make their own discoveries. As an editor of TIME FOR KIDS, she enjoys creating stories about spiders, insects, and a wider range of animals.

To Marlowe, in the hopes that he'll grow up more at ease with spiders than his mom is. —N.I.

Spiders!
Copyright © 2005 by Time Inc.
Used under exclusive license by HarperCollins Publishers Inc.
Manufactured in China by South China Printing Company Ltd.
All rights reserved. No part of this book may be used or reproduced in any manner whatsoever without written permission except in the case of brief quotations embodied in critical articles and reviews. For information address HarperCollins Children's Books, a division of HarperCollins Publishers, 1350 Avenue of the Americas, New York, NY 10019.
www.harperchildrens.com

LIBRARY OF CONGRESS CATALOGING-IN-PUBLICATION DATA

Spiders! / by the editors of Time for Kids with Nicole Iorio.— 1st ed.
p. cm. — (Time for kids science scoops)
ISBN 0-06-057634-0 (pbk.) — ISBN 0-06-057635-9 (trade)
1. Spiders—Juvenile literature. [1. Spiders.] I. Iorio, Nicole. II. Time for kids online.
III. Series.
QL458.4.S6425 2005   2003026553
595.4'4—dc22

1 2 3 4 5 6 7 8 9 10
First Edition

Copyright © by Time Inc.

TIME FOR KIDS and the Red Border Design are Trademarks of Time Inc. used under license.

Photography and Illustration Credits:
Cover: Steve Taylor—Getty Images; cover inset: John Gerlach—Animals Animals; cover front flap: Digital Vision; pp. 4–5: Kim Taylor—Bruce Coleman; pp. 6–7: Pascal Geotgheluck—AEF/Getty Images; pp. 10–11: Paul Chesley—Getty Images; pp. 12–13: Joe McDonald—Bruce Coleman; p. 13 (inset): Maria Zorn—Animals Animals; pp. 14–15: Bob Marsh—Papilio/Corbis; p. 16 (inset): Dwight Kuhn—DRK; p. 17: R.B. Suter, Vassar College; pp. 18–19: Bill Beatty; p. 20: Gladden William Willis—Animals Animals; pp. 22–23: Dag Sundberg—Getty Images; p. 25: Kevin Schafer—Corbis; pp. 26–27: Tom Bean—Getty Images; pp. 28–29: Dieter & Mary Plage—Bruce Coleman; pp. 30–31: Konrad Wothe—Minden; pp. 32–33: Satoshi Kuribayashi—OSF/DRK; p. 32 (inset): Jack Couffer—Bruce Coleman; pp. 34–35: HL Fox—OSF/Animals Animals; pp. 36–37: Scott Smith—Animals Animals; pp. 38–39: Roy Toft—National Geographic; pp. 40–41: Patricia Fogden—Corbis; p. 40 (inset): Michael Fogden—Animals Animals; pp. 42–43: Dietmar Nill—naturepl.com; pp. 44–45: Kim Taylor—Bruce Coleman; p. 44 (inset): Bill Beatty; pp. 46–47: Larry Ulrich—DRK; p. 48 (ballooning): R.B. Suter, Vassar College; p. 48 (camouflage): Scott Smith—Animals Animals; p. 48 (molt): Bill Beatty; p. 48 (sac): Bob Marsh—Papilio/Corbis; p. 48 (spiderling): Dwight Kuhn—DRK; p. 48 (deer tick): Kent Wood—Photo Researchers; p. 48 (dust mite): Andrew Syred—Photo Researchers; p. 48 (daddy longlegs): Barry Runk/Stan—Grant Heilman

Acknowledgments:
For TIME FOR KIDS: Editorial Director: Keith Garton; Editor: Nelida Gonzalez Cutler; Art Director: Rachel Smith; Photography Editor: Jill Tatara

HarperCollins books may be purchased for educational, business, or sales promotional use. For information, please write: Special Markets Department, HarperCollins Publishers Inc., 10 East 53rd Street, New York, NY 10022.

go Check us out at **www.timeforkids.com**

CONTENTS

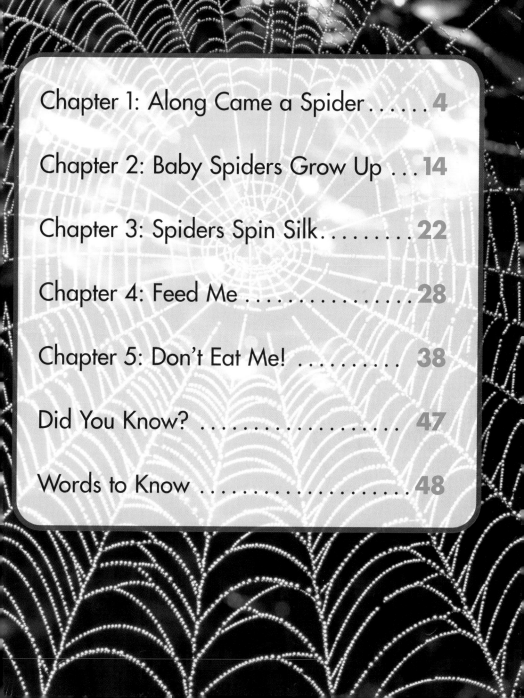

CHAPTER ONE

Along Came

Crab
spider

a Spider

You see their sticky webs. You watch them crawl on rocks and flowers. You spot them running up walls. Spiders can be black, brown, yellow, pink, and even white. Spiders come in all colors, shapes, and sizes. And spiders are full of surprises!

Don't Call Me a Bug!

Spiders are not insects.
They are arachnids (*uh-RAK-nids*). Scorpions and ticks are also arachnids. All arachnids have eight legs and two main body parts. Insects have six legs and three main body parts.

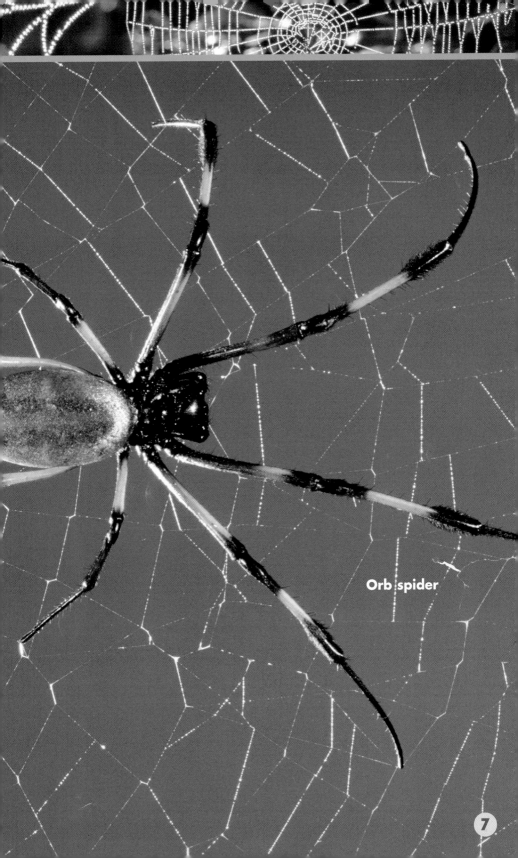

Orb spider

Take a close look at a spider.

A garden spider is an arachnid. An arachnid has two body parts: a cephalothorax (*seh-fuh-luh-THOR-ax*) and an abdomen.

CEPHALOTHORAX

It includes the head and the thorax.

spinnerets

Spiders that weave webs use these to spin silk.

eyes

Most spiders have eight eyes.

ABDOMEN

It contains a spider's important organs.

fangs

Spiders use these to inject their poison.

legs

Tiny hairs on the legs help a spider hear and smell.

Now take a close look at a fly.

A housefly is an insect. An insect has three body parts: a head, a thorax, and an abdomen.

ABDOMEN

This is the biggest body part. An insect's organs are inside it.

eyes

Some insects, like this fly, have a set of compound eyes.

THORAX

A fly's legs are attached to this middle body part.

wings

Insects that fly have wings. Some insects have wings that are thin and light. Other insects have hard wings.

legs

They help an insect walk, jump, and pick up things.

antennas

Only insects have antennas. They help the insect feel things and find food.

HEAD

The eyes, mouthparts, and antennas are on an insect's head.

Spiders are everywhere!

They are found all over the world. They can live indoors or outdoors. Spiders can live high up in trees or down under the ground. They are at home where it is cold and where it is hot.

Desert tarantulas

FRIEND OR ENEMY?

Beware! A female black widow is shiny, black, and about a half inch long. It has a red hourglass-shaped mark on its body.

An orb spider grabs a grasshopper.

Don't be scared of spiders.

Most spiders can't hurt you. Spiders are helpful. They help farmers by eating insects that harm plants.

But some are dangerous.

The black widow spider is the most dangerous kind found in the United States. A black widow that feels trapped may bite. Its poison can be very harmful. In rare cases it can be deadly. If you see a black widow, watch out!

CHAPTER TWO

Baby Spiders

A huntsman spider lays its eggs on a tree trunk.

Mother spiders can lay as many as three thousand eggs at one time. The mother lays its eggs and wraps them in a silk sac. The sac protects the eggs from heat, cold, and rain. Some spiders hide their sac to keep the eggs safe.

Wolf spider
and spiderlings

The eggs hatch.

Out come thousands of tiny baby spiders. They are called spiderlings. Most mother spiders do not stay with their babies. But some do. Wolf spiders carry their babies on their backs.

Spiderlings spread out to find food. Some go ballooning! They climb up high and drop into the air on long lines of silk.

The wind picks up the silk threads and takes the spiderlings for a ride. Each baby spider finds a new home.

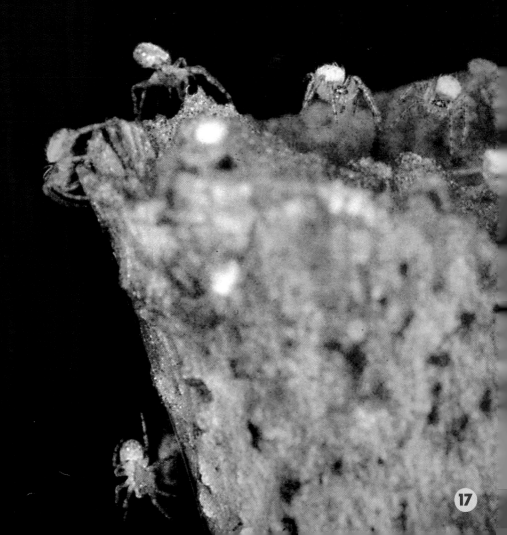

It took this hunting
spider hours to shed
the old outside layer
of its body.

Time for a change!

As they grow, spiders get too big for their skin and shed the outside layer. This is called molting. They replace the outside layer with a new layer. Spiders keep molting until they become the size they will stay as adults. A spider molts about five to ten times in its life.

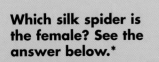

Which silk spider is the female? See the answer below.*

THE FEMALE IS THE BIG SPIDER ON THE RIGHT.*

Many spiders change their color or shape as they grow.

Some spiders in the same family grow bigger than others. Most female spiders are bigger than male spiders.

How Big?

Many kinds of spiders can fit inside your hand.

But some like the Goliath tarantula are as big as a dinner plate!

Others like the Samoan moss spider are as tiny as the point of a pencil.

CHAPTER THREE

Spiders Spin

A spider makes silk inside its body. The silk comes out at the back tip. The spider then uses its spinnerets like fingers to spin the silk into thread. Spider silk can be fluffy, tough, or sticky. Sticky silk helps trap insects.

Silk

Spider silk is super strong!

It is nature's strongest fiber. It is even stronger than steel. Spider silk is also super stretchy. It is more elastic than a rubber band.

How Far?

A silk thread can stretch across fifty feet without breaking. That means it could reach all the way across a basketball court!

This ogre-faced spider is making a net from silk. It will toss the net at an insect.

Spiders use their silk in many ways.

This orb spider is making a web with silk. It takes a spider less than an hour to spin a web—even a complex one!

CHAPTER FOUR

Feed Me

Spiders hunt in many ways. Not all spiders weave webs. But some spiders are experts at weaving them. They catch food in their webs. Then they wait until an insect lands on the sticky silk. It's lunchtime!

An orb spider wraps a fly in a web.

GOTCHA!

Grass spiders spin funnel webs.
The web is wide at the top and narrow at
the bottom. The spider waits for its food
to drop right in.

How Big?

Social spiders are found in South America. They can work together to make a giant web that covers a tree!

Spiders use many tricks to hunt their food.

The trapdoor spider digs a hole in the ground. It covers the hole with a door that is made out of dirt. Then it waits underground. When an insect walks by, out pops the spider!

POUNCE!

The jumping spider has great eyesight. When it spots a tasty bug, the spider jumps into the air. *Pounce!* Dinner is served.

Water spiders go fishing for their food.

The water spider dives underwater and builds a web inside a bubble. Then it uses its legs like a fishing pole to pull in insects, tadpoles, and even small fish.

Some spiders play hide-and-seek with their food. They use camouflage. The crab spider blends in with the flowers it sits on. When an insect lands on a flower, it doesn't see the spider. This bumblebee is in for a real surprise!

CHAPTER FIVE

Don't Eat Me!

Spiders have many predators. Birds, snakes, frogs, wasps, crickets, and lizards all eat spiders. Spiders have many ways to escape their enemies. They hurry off into tunnels or sail away on their silk threads. But some predators are too quick and catch the spiders!

Spiders are tasty snacks to lizards like this one.

Watch it roll!

When a wheel spider gets scared, it tucks in its legs. It escapes its enemies by rolling across the sand.

A fisher spider gets away by walking on water.

It tiptoes lightly across the water.
Its waxy legs don't even get wet.

One spider and two ants are in this picture. Can you tell which is which? See the answer below.*

Some spiders are copycats.

Their bodies are shaped like other things. The ant mimic spider has the same shape and color as an ant. The spider's enemies are fooled. They pass right by the disguised spider.

*THE SPIDER IS IN THE MIDDLE.

The shape of a spider can also warn off predators. Some spiders have long, sharp spikes on their bodies. A bird would have a hard time eating this spiny spider.

Meet a Real Spider-Man

Steven Kutcher gets paid to play with spiders. That's why he loves his job! Kutcher is a scientist who studies insects and spiders. He also works on movies. When moviemakers need creepy crawlers for a movie, they call Kutcher. He picked out the spiders that were used in *Spider-Man*.

When Kutcher was a kid, he was scared of tarantulas. But he's not afraid of them anymore. "When you learn about something, the fear goes away," he says. Now Kutcher keeps fifty spiders as pets. An orange-knee tarantula is one of his favorites.

Did You Know?

- Spiders make seven kinds of silk.

- The web of a golden silk spider is strong enough to trap a bird.

- Some spiders eat their webs and then reuse them.

- When a spider sinks its fangs into an insect, poison flows into the insect's body.

- Spiders have two main eyes that are used for seeing. The other eyes are sensitive to light and shadow.

WORDS to Know

Arachnid: an animal group that includes spiders, scorpions, mites, and ticks

Molt: to shed the h[ard] outside layer [of] the body

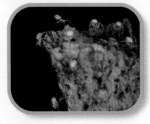

Ballooning: when spiders are carried in the wind by their silk threads

Sac: a bag or pouch; spide[rs] wrap their eg[gs] in a silk sac

Camouflage: to blend in with the surroundings

Spiderli[ng] a baby spide[r]

FUN FACTS **MEET OTHER ARACHNIDS**

Deer tick

Dust mite

White scorpion

Daddy longlegs